T0328498

Star Reverse

Star Reverse

by

Linda Ann Strang

DRYAD PRESS

People! Read Poetry

Star Reverse

Dryad Press (Pty) Ltd
Postnet Suite 281, Private Bag X16, Constantia, 7848,
Cape Town, South Africa
www.dryadpress.co.za/business@dryadpress.co.za

Editor: Michèle Betty
Copy Editor: Helena Janisch
Cover design & typography: Stephen Symons
Set in 9.5/14pt Palatino Linotype
First published in Cape Town by Dryad Press (Pty) Ltd, 2022

ISBN 978-1-991209-13-9 (Print)
ISBN 978-1-991209-14-6 (Electronic)

Visit www.dryadpress.co.za to read more about all our books and to buy
them. You will also find features, links to author interviews and news of
author events. Follow our social media platforms on Instagram and Facebook
to be the first to hear about our new releases.

Dryad Press is supported by the Government of South Africa through the
National Arts Council of South Africa (an agency of the Department of Arts &
Culture), whose assistance is gratefully acknowledged.

for my son, Dillon Mostert,
with all the love and music

CONTENTS

I Zubenelhakrabi

A Song for a Moment of Silence   3
A Brief Biography of the Opposite of Night   5
Marc and a New Theory of Moment   6
Troy in the Cancer Ward   7
Isolde Underground   9
Méliés, the Moon Has No Money   10
Nocturne with Light Pollution, Poets and Fruit Bats   12
Seaward   13
Sea of Trees: Aokigahara   14
Hallucination on the Road to Kuruman   16
Enteric-Coated Nightmare 45   18

II Vega

A Brief History of Shadows, a Natural History
of the Night Before   23
Visions in a Drought   25
Everything's Real Somewhere, They Say   27
Dystopia with Benefits   28
Mr and Mrs Noah Nova   30
Surreal Housekeeping, Good Advice   32
With Vinegar and Brown Paper   34
The Subject by Multiple Choice   36
Héloïse in Hell   37

III Tislit

Hook's DIY in a Hard Father's Workshop   43
Table Setting with Willow Pattern Plates   45
Digesting Childhood   46

The Starveling Anthology   47
Mother and Child Understory   49

IV Capella

Kleptoglade   53
Leaf Encounter   54
Op Art   55
Leda and the Dream Lily   56
Midnight Metro with Anaïs Nin   57

V Betelgeuse

Miriam Splitting   61
Morphine Ward on Psychiatric Fire   63
Findhorn Fly Fishing: Eternal Damnation   64
The Boutique Hotel: A Dream   65
A Song from the Land of Collage   66
Little One Eye and the Cyclops   67
Equinox Ego   68

VI Antares

Song of the Émigré   73
Nemesis Depressed   74
The Angel Gabriel Advises the Rebel Leader   76
The Woman Ravaged Meditates on Hard   77
Three Spirits That Follow the Comet of Anguish   79
Philomela Unravels Nigeria   80
Butterfly Djinn   81
The Sky of Women: China   82
Syrian Villanelle   83
Nagasaki Deconstructed   84

Acknowledgements   86
End Notes   87

I

Zubenelhakrabi

A Song for a Moment of Silence

What female heart
can guilt despise?
What night's averse
to stars?

The way Ben E. King looks
to mountains that humble.
The way that the mountains
go west without breathing.

I've handcuffed myself
to the absence of heartbeat,
ricochet roses,
a thrice-broken window.

This is the man
in the bonfire moon.
The memory raking,
the tongues of cold flame.

This is the scar
of my Rhett down the drain,
the past I can't let
through the ribs of a keyhole.

Glance into surgery,
tunnels of light,
nettings of suture,
the fish from the ceiling.

I'd like to retain
all your strokes as reward.
Death stretches, a black cat
that sleeps in the ward.

The gold of your laughter,
clatters in Libra –
purring old fur's
on the way to the funeral –

so, this is the songline
at risk in my wrists.
Come lick at the prayer
that I've pulsed in my fists.

A Brief Biography of the Opposite of Night

If light were you,
would you go through my body like a flare
when I throw open the doors of the cathedral,
kiss my eyes, my hair, as I stand on the crest of the steps
above the square? Would you play through the lace
of my dress, a barely perceptible glow on my breasts?
Could your happiness best be expressed through the blue
of a Chartres window?

If light had a wife,
would her name be Wavelength,
suggesting crests and surfing at sunset?
Would she give him a rollercoaster kind of life
or would it be all over the rainbow? Would he end his days
herding indigo goats though canyons of ultraviolet
for a few groats, red dust staining the hems of his coat?

If light were a little girl
with broken shoes, would she go alone between the stars,
year after year, fostered by white dwarves
who couldn't keep her?
Would she weep on the wide highway
past Cassiopeia, dropping golden daisies
into the chasms of the night?

And when you wish upon them, my dear,
do you wish with all your might?

Marc and a New Theory of Moment

Lovers do levitate as depicted by Chagall,
but only after a spectacular accident:
a motorcycle crash, a train off track,
an airplane exploding on impact, perhaps.
After the bad aster comes a circus hush
as the lovers rise above the rest of us.

If you don't blink, you can see them smiling
on a trapeze as trite as a V of geese.
They gaze enraptured at the flow of moments,
taste angel food cake, wear long velvet gloves,
play Chinese checkers, fast and loose, swinging
on gamely for the sake of love – and, carelessly,
they swear that until death do them part
they will live in mid-air.

Then the lion tamer loses his head.
A scream flaps away with the tent.
The lovers fall as we fret.
The lovers fall. There's no net.

The spectators forsake all silence –
and the helicopter doctors come in
with their coats, and their goats, and their violins.

Troy in the Cancer Ward

Such a Greek gift this cancer is,
inside your body, crone artefact.

Cronus, chemo, metastasis,
a blade taking time in your breast,

adulterers flogged, our family sacked.
Poseurs and posies, pollen spilt,

demon drops, lemon drops, alveoli,
arteries garotted and bled.

All the unholy mysteries
confessed to the oxygen mask,

thermometer no sweet to suck on.
The spectres of every defile,

still wounded, appear at this bed.
Odysseus under the ribcage,

white with rage, the night
claustrophobic with heroes.

Opiates the prize and the purse,
every breath a humid distress.

Assault nurses repress the pressure,
anything to halt the rocking. Bit

again, Vitruvian toy. Reaper
on a hobby. Bolts. This is the death

rattle chincherinchee. Iron maiden.
Hoarse. Feathermen. Bring me my colt.

Isolde Underground

~ Isolde Underground

A busker husks   his feet in the subway,
guitar overturned,   snifter riffs on their heads,

two discarded socks.   He lights a cigarette,
dreaming of St Just,   and Clovelly perhaps.

Rye. He stands,   his own peninsula.
Tristan alone.   Rebel. The colour of sails a test.

Solo naked, whisky   fumes, cologne. Isolde
in a black coat,   Walkman, stops.

Departing King's   Cross, takes the songs
(shelter – storm –   on the tracks)

up the stairs,   blonde hair, no cares.
In love   for two streets,

she missed   by moments the igniting,
the damned.   *That honeysuckle*
hazel girl?   The one with white hands.

Méliès, the moon has no money

not even a sixpence –
she rolls in the gutter like a rotten orange.

The moon was a modest movie star, pliant,
musky but silent. Debutantes fainted
to the sound of pianos.

Along the Champs Élysées – Paris in ostrich,
depressed – she was numinous,

she lost luminous gloves.
Everyone there felt obscurely caressed.

The moon loves frottage.
Her tears stand erect on the dark side
of the tram although her laughs are full of light.

Like one of the elect,
she alights with four-and-twenty blackbirds.
Baked in a pie, they birth themselves

with bloody beaks,
bursting through a flaky pastry sky.

Bulimic? The moon is.
She devours chocolate out of the night
and retches into the ocean's toilet.

She's a gem.
I have my finger down the moon's throat.
She has my pulse in her brain stem.

She's eaten by wolves, clawed at by owls.
Her howls, melodic, escape from their mouths.

The moon covers mothers in pale sheets.
They hover and fret, humidifying ghosts.
There stands one at the foot of your bed.

I always contemplate the moon at midnight.
Later, I grate her for breakfast with chives.

She draws all my madness out,
like a poultice with two black eyes,
like a magnet wearing a dirty white dress.

Nocturne with Light Pollution, Poets and Fruit Bats

Fitzgerald and Keats get pissed in a dive bar,
the night pinches stars in the purse of its lips.

I try to find straws and some shades to believe in –
my empty field is a room with a bed.

Light is the night and tender it isn't.
Hey, big spender, won't you go down on me?

The slut moths, insane with their scorch and delusion,
catcall to a moon that, all poppy, gives head.

Oh, to nurse and guide broken bodies through nectar –
not star-averse perfume of torture and burn.

Light is the night and without doubt not tender:
the dying and mist are not ever fêted.

Bats in leather jackets, on a sorry wind farm,
lie rigid and bloody. The turbines that loved them

are windmills that flail like stiff human beings.
In alleys with jasmine, all condoms and drowning,

we attempt to find heaven when lost out at sea.

Seaward

They say this was a fishing village once.
On the homeward commute, we identify with driftwood,

tight-knit communities underneath our eyelids,
sponges heavy with unshed weeping.

Pillow books hidden behind the billboards –
Genji, haiku, French letters and shells –

the only tide is the ebb on our pay cheques.
At the stations, we can feel the oceans quiver –

behind the containers and the tungsten lighting,
gunmetal gulls and a deal winter's day.

Neuralgia needling all along our cheekbones,
one more shift and the seabed could rupture –

muted cries in our hallways, only voices of ghosts.
The waves wash up behind a ten-storey building.

Waves in their wisdom have stories themselves.

Underneath our bandages are brittle stars.
Hidden in our splints are bleeding birds.

Come here and you can taste the sea word.

Sea of Trees: Aokigahara

Should you ever climb
the cone in winter,

this is what you'd see below:
spirit foxes at charades

pulling faces in the snow –
not the lurid ghosts of summer.

Stomach contents, nitrogen,
adventitious, tap, the dead,

mossy sockets, razor cuts,
fledglings mum inside the head.

Creeping lettuce, hearts of darts,
fern brakes full of blood.

Fuji Maiko, my kimono girl,
on her hip one hairstreak,

a twisted queue her back
(sinuous, the human whip at night),

her naked spine,
hot beads of headlights.

With my spinel eyes, I climb
to claim her oxygen

starvation. Suicide-
inclined night wife, rewind,

above the spinney
of forgotten foreheads,

rope burn ...
the love of my life.

Hallucination on the Road to Kuruman

Tourists, a desert road is the tongue
of chameleon, ant bear – endless –
and the road rolls up
when you least expect it.

Your campfire's a gasp in the night,
though you share your *dagga* with the devil,
his goat eyes prolonging the pleasure
above a burning marrow-bone pipe.

Another day dawns with visits
to cow-dung cathedrals,
floors polished with ox blood –
pampelmoes, slave bells,

shafts of sunlight and bats in the rafters.
See scorpion ciphers, adder Morse,
a bush with berries
called white woman's breasts.

At last, reaching water, you'll swim
but realise every puddle's
been poisoned by the Mantis –
who moulded mankind

from the fly-kissed carcasses
of impala. Kudu crania pale
in dusk, sepia telegraphs,
rain turns away

at the side of the sky. A scarecrow
looks down through a visor of locusts.
When every outcry crackles with static,
what besides stones can you purchase?

Enteric-Coated Nightmare 45

45
times the music box dancer
with spinal cancer.

Mesmerise me with tutu.
Tulle. Close my eyes.

45
sotto in su. Clouds. Both sides
of the sternum now.

45
I lift up my eyes to forget-me-not,
mass production horses framed.

Running cobalt, falling water,
Mammy ... key blue.

II

Vega

A Brief History of Shadows, a Natural History of the Night Before

Were the shadows
in the snowfields really lavender
as Pushkin pushed off in ermine,
la-la-ing his love poems alone?

Can you view through the skyline
Ansel Adams and Pollux?
Oh, stop, it was Lawrence.
Oh no, it was nightshift.

Manhattan's entirely upside
down in a dew drop,
sticking tail cock softly
to corolla plumbago.

A shadow has a Saturn sense
of humour, slavering plangent
for the noose in your purse.
The violins that play

in the welt of dead Carthage,
the overnight oat fields
you spilt – all spelt in the velvet
deeps of a cicada car seat.

Shadows are filigree brushdance
below Zen zero snowdrops.
Subtly spiced with Arabian
midnight tulip in sherbet, Dido,

kohl delicate, lowered
under Côte Demure
landscapes of Lamia, lashes
the memory lid.

Toto floating. Pearls
are famous for their fear of shadows.
Name them id husk
when fainting.

Shadows undertake a staccato tango
behind your plosives
when you fib about the beast
you breathed in last night.

Lock your indigo shadows in an ivory box.
They are hardly contained.
Their tales are hidden in the fox of your hand.

Of late, rabble rabbits burble out of matinee
wrists. Hunch pack, they hop away
obliquely, live mysterious lives.

Visions in a Drought

My ex-husband and my ex-father
are engaged to the rain gauge.

Today I have become a granadilla,
withered, my skin pitted and cracked.

Even the agave has given up.
There are no mescaline epiphanies

in the Kalahari, no amusing mirages
in the ochre above. No geode is bursting

with magnificent God. The sky tastes of dust.
Paint is peeling all over the desert,

a bitter pill – my placebo for love.
Caprivi, strip because everything's naked,

the sun's carnal knowledge
in the corps of our bones.

The terrified stars see their long hair on fire,
their tresses fall on the earth in ash.

My salt rose is burning.
My armpits are charred.

Agave Maria, the poison bush weeps,
the lions pick up my bones like sticks.

Forgive them, my lavender snakebite,
my Cleopatra pitter patter.

Despite the night ocean,
gelignite shattering the trachea, tripe,

offal – jackal benedictions,
please give them respite.

Everything's Real Somewhere, They Say

Rowena Leila, poor relation, tongue-tied at a birthday tea
Along grey sedge, a golden swan surveys the glitter hunters

sees six women bonding with articulate eyebrows –
whose arrows are aimed at her clairvoyant neck.

lace, éclairs, and red velvet cake – not to mention funnel.
Through wormholes of diamond she deftly escapes.

Overseas travel, Princeton children, obvious success:
On a planet far away, all are punished with death,

they buzz like wasps inside a lily's fragrant head.
yet a woman with wings is flying through lead, noble.

Invisible, the sun begins to set. Who is to guess
In mutable multiverses, swans may be lilies, a lamb,

she sacrificed two months of meat to buy a decent dress?
circles, a turtle, a willow, a wisp, a manifestation

The hostess Candice gives her own Chanel a sly caress, rises
on eight spider legs, a rocking horse, Io, a packet of pegs.

soignée, inviting her éclat of guests to admire
Her feather arms, here empty, in another world embrace

her wisteria flowers that do not exist, nor weeping
with joy a youth who plays a lyre, fingers on fire, in truth …

children, in Universe One Thousand, except as a myth.

Dystopia with Benefits

A telephone rings in my Christmas uterus.
Should I answer it? A yellow fish dives into a pyramid

of pearls on the mantelpiece. We are no longer girls.
There's a ship made of gin and cocaine in the kitchen.

A gingerbread past. I'm lashed to the mast.
I'm regnant with pay-as-you-go. I'm pregnant

and made out of calico – under a dazing chain
in the mist of the midst of menopause. A daisy tsunami

of encores from the past pours through my
window. But for me, no more fandango. No more

sin. Too much information. Too much chin chin.
Too much dogged and dogging Rin Tin Tin.

Some wit in your Twitter? I would pay you
in kind. I would pay you in groin. But twenty

elephants climb out of my coin. When I waltz,
take my pulse. I've become the false Bottom

I always hoped I would find. I choose ears
for my avatars. Can't you see that I'm blind?

I can't function. Nevertheless, I have: less
Oberon, more unction; an air, a grace, an air bag,

a windbag, a second face. Give me lights for the tree.
Give me volts for the flex. The angel, in coal tar

and tinsel, swings by her neck. Here's a *like* from my ex –
a balm for my scars – and a text from Hansel, an SOS,

his blood on the sextant, under marzipan far-distant stars.

Mr and Mrs Noah Nova

retire and buy a houseboat,
nouveau riche in ostriches
and other flightless birds.
She secretly trains two circus fleas
with stag beetles for extras.
What an act and what a trapeze!

With hymns to Rachel Carson in heaven,
the evening affords a doggy coupling
with Mr Noah the night rhinoceros,
the hyenas high and the glow worms low.
Then it's gin for breakfast
with a bowl of elvers, margaritas
and a juniper dove.

They take to fondling one another
in public. He cups her breast
while an ibis looks on.
They have toe rings, ring tones,
rose tattoos, a white bowler hat.
Mr Noah affects a polka dot cravat,
Mrs Noah a boa constrictor.

They learn high-stakes poker,
qigong, gun running,
not-on-your-nelly belly dancing
and publish the proof on Facebook.

So, their children sequester a pea-green boat,
taking Magellan as a *nom de guerre*,
muttering things like *For crying out loud*,
forsaking the owl and the pussy cat,
brandishing tallow and a swizzle stick,
they set sail for another cloud.

Surreal Housekeeping, Good Advice

Dear Leonora, Remedios and Max,

What plants are easy to grow inside?

Avid Gardener

    * * *

Dear Avid,

The seeds of certain fruit trees, if swallowed,
are said to grow inside the gut.
Symptoms may include a halo of apricots.

The vanilla vandals inside your mouth
are only bumbling bees, my dear.
Gorilla gardening is a last resort.

After shaping a swan song,
you may pierce the ear.
An ear is an apiary every head should sport.

Love Leonora

    * * *

Dear Gardener,

Give ear to me. I grew inside a gravid peach,
a cherub instead of a grub – ectopic mother
cut me free and showered me with love.

My grandmother cultivated cast iron plants, sadly,
inside her breasts. She only wanted to avoid the fist.
She only wanted to endure the dust.

Remedios Varo

* * *

Dear me!

Self-examine for Buddhist Pine, Wandering Jew,
Zebrina, and even Pineapple Antlers.
Get a medical opinion. Ignore the Nazi answer.

M.E.

With Vinegar and Brown Paper

Jesus said, *The man you are now with*
is not your husband.
The well you are plumbing with him will give
no pail full of love nor a Jack
to go back down the hill with when you attend
the spectacle of my crucifixion come Easter.

No one to hold your hand
at the hotdog stands –
not to mention the vegetarian pizzas.

The truth is you have had many husbands
and, though you're on the shelf,
they're in movie houses, big brass beds
or even gondolas with someone else.
But who am I to judge?

By the way, here's his lawful wedded wife
with a social worker and the local preacher,
verily. They want a word
and they won't budge.

The woman – who (unlike some)
could not summon sweet Brent Crude
or wishes fulfilled from the well –
realised then it's hard to tell Jesus
from the devil or even Bob Dylan.

Anyway, the die was cast; the coin was flipped.
The bastard fruit of her womb
rolled over and slept.
Jesus put a starry harpoon to his lips and winked.
The woman wept.

The Subject by Multiple Choice

1. The subject deserves:
   a) all B's
   b) all C's
   c) D minus or even an E

2. Because, metaphorically speaking, her marriage was:
   a) that stink worm Leviathan in the kitchen sink
   b) a shift to the violet end of the spectrum
   c) a violence case study carved on a plectrum
   d) none of the above

3. Rate her kisses. When she kisses she's like:
   a) burning swigs of bourbon
   b) a Gelli plate patterned ermine
   c) an anglepoise glow
   d) Robin Hood in a leather jerkin
   e) I do not know

4. She could improve herself if she opened:
   a) a packet of false eyelashes for her nondescript eyes
   b) the zipper of her sheep disguise
   c) the Edinburgh tattoo, singing the blues
   d) *He's Just Not That Into You*
   e) *Powers of Horror* and *The Wings of a Dove*

5. Do you think she should choose the following?
   Answer yes or no.

   f) all of the above

Héloïse in Hell

Appalled behind pear trees, impeached,
espaliered against the brick,
crows on the nunnery wall,
dog's mercury under my feet …

Hark the incubus hidden within,
angel-faced codling moth deep in my womb.
With what serpents have you been pleached?
ring the bells of Lauds and Compline.

There goes Sister Ebba – unseen,
so she thinks – feeding the finches or elves
with crumbs we could have eaten ourselves.
Our petty rule has been breached.

A purple frog hopping upon the garth
pulses like Abelard's member –
severed. I'm a friend to Nebuchadnezzar.
We'll swallow the greensward together.

Abelard claims he didn't love me.
He swears he doesn't remember.
But he drew out my sword-like pleasure.
Libations of wine on my breasts –

he kissed them and said they were blessed –
while in the forest outside wolves wept.
His breath was the Spirit of God
stoking the back of my neck.

We rode out at full moon, hot leather,
my side-saddle glittered with sweat,
stars fell like snow from the sky,
a tarragon rosemary track,

a wynd that led to the sea,
his hand on the small of my back,
more debauchery. Naked as a fisher boy
I washed away his seed. A wave splashed.

Once at Michaelmas, miracle plays,
mummery, Abelard touched my hand. Thorns
for the lost and sad. Rats in the straw.
Life has become like that.

Sister Ebba, did you really hide
crumbs in your ravening sleeves?
How itchy. Whatever shall the Abbess say?
Oh yes, of course – that's me.

III

Tislit

Hook's DIY in a Hard Father's Workshop

The captain there, I swear, he's in love with a saw
tuning in circular to songs of a wounding.
But the saw, I see, has designs on a hand plane.

Plainer, of course, though she has her appeal,
lolling with Safety Pin Up Girl '95
beside cobweb, sawdust, lawyer's letters, knives.

I will not parley with the spirit level.
I will make no metaphor that you need to unscrew.
But then I know how to talk through a parallel jaw.

A gang of planks leans up against the wall.
The planks may be lost boys or no boys at all.

Captain Hook flirts, only briefly, with wing nuts –
an after effect of that business with fairies –

recalls Peter bleeding through juvenile hall.
In a reverie of tick tocks,
he knocks over white paint. Coming in colours

like Cream, Duck Egg, Fig Slut, Pain Sob,
and Bone. Houses painted never – never – are rainbows.

The gang that is spanked regresses to fir trees.
The boys dream of needle pine kisses, the narc.
The paint dreams of flying over London with solvent.

Please support, implicitly, National Simper Day.
Please import, implicitly, little girls and their pockmarks.

Please deport, explicitly, divorced children, the park.
Report, with duplicity, our home in the tree roots.

The chipmunks near the fountain are wearing red jackets.
In the closet? Yes, but please let's not go there.

They stow away tenon and chamfer for winter.
They stash, for holocausts, birdcage and scratch. Tinker,

what kind of theatre do you watch through an eye patch?

Table Setting with Willow Pattern Plates

What was her name, this sketch girl arrested,
hand painted daughter caught running,
her life under two birds abridged?

She haunts my dreams,
my antique shagreen,
this child of a tea tray,

trade routes, gunpowder –
tripping through the doorway
on malformed feet,

wearing cheongsams, peonies
and frogging. A golden lily
by any other name, like torture

for instance, would smell as sweet.
Now, her head under glaze is at rest,
diffident for all the guests,

submissive to lamb as to soup,
cherry trees blue in the bisque,
her father still wielding a whip.

Digesting Childhood

Even now I can hear the broken wings
in the sordid deeps of the bear –
protein feature, double denature,
the silver scream, the creamy teenager,
the tanager screen.

At eight, I built a secret house
out of candy cane Reader's
Digest. Hung upside down
on the loops of the sun
till a witch came along like Your Highness.

Every wooden block has newsflash
hidden, microscopic, inside it. Tarot
bookmark the flaming tower –
Mother, the puzzle, she kicked it.

The bear wakes up, picks its teeth
with our erstwhile and white picket fence –
coughs up cakes, Alka-Seltzer lakes,
charges the meridian rent.

Deep vein Elm Street – *Run, don't walk.*
The knife gets away with pep talk.
The little cops lag to see such fun. I lie.
I digest a dish of die in the dark.

The Starveling Anthology

Here the woman is: no bra,
herpes, tsetse, abscess, teeth.

She decides to broil the deceased raw priest's
cut-out poetry. Her children, starving,

spend their days playing – pluck naked –
with phantom bantams

and dreams of plantains. Into the cauldron,
quatrains – unknowable things.

First to the air in steam:
pictogram, apse and *purpurine.*

Next, the reworking of chemical bonds,
configurations forged in heat:

delphinium synagogue billowing,
firefly bezique, Milky Way tentacle,

turpentine peacock, rose of dusted sugar
nightstick, nacre galliard undersong,

peachy cravat yoni kiss.
A whiff of *chardonnay hibiscus*

makes the infants drool and weep.
The boiling over of *angels,*

moonlight, lakes and *love* is fated.
But served up, the pages are tasteless,

a pap that makes the family retch.
No flowers. A pot of iron, their mother scours.

Mother and Child Understory

In my feral fantasies
of American hemlock,
you should have been born
in Olympic Park:
amber manoeuvres

of butterflies felt
through amniotic fluid;
child of a fiddlehead,
dogwoods, ardour,
rhododendron, dog star, other;

moss on the rocks
to mattress my travail,
volcanic sand
beneath my fingernails.
All the living must rise above

the lochia-scented layette of blood –
then received by yttrium,
and other rare earths, the afterbirth.
Hummingbirds to fan your face,

bright-eyed beadles,
fern vernix the bed,
butterfly midwives –
my Hades princess.

IV

Capella

Kleptoglade

daffinfidel to be hidden in honeyquill
to walk all William sweetrap
in treebelle and   bluebraille
become the lurkblur
of the blurtrain
                in larkspa and veilvert

for musicsot and dovemot
come to lightanemone
Gethsemane

frailblossom
pearlitter

                Gentmyrrh of Ophir
my plangentian
fallow lantburn

Leaf Encounter

Forgive the forest, so seldom relaxed –
river of tannin, occasion for breathing,

a slipknot of rushes, a fountain ahead,
wellspring into which you can whisper

your hunger for slippery slopes.
A foxglove worth hunting, a tongue with a touch

of comeliest Latin. In time, not a stitch,
no guilt, no reproach. For each golden sailor,

an ocean of fleece. For you citronella,
for you rose of attar. One brief encounter –

inter alia glossolalia –

certainly has too short a lease. Cinnamon-centred
Pentecost of the lost? Isle of the Blest?

Lap up my luxury? Venery, yes.

Op Art

We become the pitch
of opium,

magnetic lechery of iron
filings, skin

all seersucker,
firelings,

mammilla mantic;
tectonic strata,

unstable planet,
contour lines drifting

agate by agate.
Banded on bandit,

all fingerprint pattern,
we net each other in

for deeper delirium.
Then we're Cossack on zebra,

barred and confessing,
tigers undressing,

scored out stars
and isobars –

venetian blinds tracking
all that kissing.

Leda and the Dream Lily

Once he touched her wrist by accident
and left a dint of birdsong, like a lantern,
thin as a petal, in her tendon.

So, as she falls asleep this night,
she rebuffs the demons
who rise up to greet her, embraces instead

a calla disguised as her lover; notices that the lily
is not only white, but roué rouge and creole ochre,
hardly sees whether her lover is man and woman,

or either, or neither. But, licking the spadix,
gives herself over to cream and ether, her hips
lapping gently as a lake full of ripples on the bed.

Her dreams ascend, fulsome as all seven swans
in the neck of her womb, as she leans forward
with her other mouth, to swallow

the swan sound and the honey spoon.

Midnight Metro with Anaïs Nin

A fire fie fisting trick
tripping in the skin.
Cinder from a dream train,
heat in the ravine.

Music of the gem
spinet hidden in a bead.
Nerve's cream, echo wing,
honey bud, pepper comb,

vibrissa dove, starry night,
Melissa fur, fever bone.
Throw me a bird, burr belly –
I'll fly you back home.

V

Betelgeuse

Miriam Splitting

Her diamond's a mind that bursts like a light bulb: epic, inept
and etched onto windowpanes around the world,
reflecting rainbows through nail clippings –

blue girls in dog paintings.

She declares, *A daffodil's calculus to the yellow divorced. Cry,*
revived triumphant in spring. I'm mute
as a crepe fruit.

Faded neighbours say, *Schizo.*

Man damn, don't believe her. She collapses … into nocturnes
in the city library, hears moonlight arabesques
dripping with honey. She slides,

all spine, riding Morocco. Rococo.

Then come visions of starlings and rumpled Richelieu, issuing
from Shakespeare. Defecating on Thomas Love Peacock,
they fix her with grainy gazes of garret,

discourse upon Plato.

With a flurry of wings, they burrow wormholes and wombs
at the back of the books. They tell her to shush,
though their echoing voices (Richelieu's too)

chatter in congress from PL to S.

The pansy-pressed librarian wears a red fez. Head undressed,
on a platter, Miriam says, *I'm undefeated, unimpressed.*
But when she walks by the river,

the river heaves its breasts.

Miriam sees kingfishers in the reeds wearing cilices, stinging
flies hitting home, and then beside her – reigning – a girl
with earthmover eyes and tourmaline skin:

grinning – off key – singing.

Morphine Ward on Psychiatric Fire

Pyrefighters, Jacob's ladders,
roger me to burnt out *playa*.

Laocoön python girl's
cartoon in frontal bathrobe –

sucking on the beryl asp,
demented like a sweetscope.

Hope says, please
light please. Vomit a

Thermopylae mommeter.
Waltzers in a purple haze,

turn butterflies
high to May Day blue.

Handcuffs burn, O,
Whiskey Tango.

My Ripley wrists.
My pinafore wits.

Lovebird nurses,
boscage brows,

goatheards of Gethsemane,

opioids, for me alone,
foxtrot an open window.

Findhorn Fly Fishing: Eternal Damnation

Nymph larvae are available down below.

Devils crack our heads open, with wisecracks about it.
I swear there were eider ducks here on a Sunday.

On the rocks near the Satan church, the weather is sulphur,
Let's cast invicta. No? Woolly bugger myself.

Deuteronomy neutered. The demons have bangles
They were so funny. Eccles. Secombe. Black bun

and furies flip our eyes for omelettes. Scalping,
for picnics. Sculpin! Here are leeches, matches.

they're Chernobyl brambles that won't go away.
So, how many noble ways to catch the trout?

Fish poison, dynamite, cannot be counted.
My nerve ends are thousands of elders on fire.

Panfish, muddler, dace, deceiver…
Help me, Styx, I've lost control of my movements.

The Boutique Hotel: A Dream

Every time you turn left, you wear a new outfit
but don't be conceited. There is no red carpet.

The waitress serves up liquor of lilac. Petula Clark
is a crooning petunia. She has an attack of lark

echolalia. Her microphone vaults right over the bellhop
saying, *Come on, Lois, you can give us a high note.*

So you cry out, *Gideons, please help me, I'm sorry.*
For unlocking hell, you need karaoke.

The chandeliers fall, fermenting your trench coat.
The charge of the light brigade shrinks to a mobile.

You send SOS's: *My darling, my cutthroat ...*
There's breakfast all day if you're open all night.

And Mae West's breasts if you shoot her on sight.
In your maple syrup suite, Galatea likes grabbing

the sheets. She has a case full of samples. Giving teat,
and ample, a Cyclops will sing you to sleep.

A Song from the Land of Collage

Madness is life in the land of collage –
our tender feelings are just a mirage.

Machete Girl's boiling some *papier-mâché*,
and into her pot go Cocteau and Genet.

Magazine cuttings are starting to breathe.
Refined kitchen sugar can bubble and seethe.

She debones the chick with the corseted waistline.
Bonne Année aches in the frowns of your headline.

My jugular's caught in the typeset for terror
and under your apple a *sans serif* error

says, *My darling Adam, please don't never leave her.*
Mercury's message denotes only fever.

My face is all red with reports from the Bourse.
Saint Paul has been cast from his frame and the horse.

My home's filling up with the paper doll dead.
Jennifer Jones lies down flat in the shed.

Some cellophane highlights my paper angina.
The Constable's dressed in ten transfers for china.

Machete Girl pastes on some scenes from *Aladdin*
and gives you three gift tags, the heads of our children.

Little One Eye and the Cyclops

In the authentic version, Little One Eye
is the persecuted heroine
with her empire dress and a bearded iris
in the middle of her forehead.
So many curls. Horrid, horrid.

One Eye loves the boy next door
who is a Cyclops with a taste for war.
But her swain desires fair Galatea
and, plainly, One Eye tends to spy
while he satiates her.

Little One Eye becomes obsessed,
always peeping instead of action,
her pupil dilating – stubborn attraction –
her lashes flickering to the point of distraction,
while Little Two Eyes and Little Three Eyes
grow fat on goat's milk, lamb and French fries.

One Eye becomes as thin as the thrill
of a battle hymn sung across the hill
in the middle of the night.
No wonder when Napoleon comes to town
she becomes his ensign, cuts the girls into quarters –

weeps over her folly, untold waters.
Then she drums the horses and the magical dogs
all the way to Waterloo,
her heart as tender as a tinderbox –
their eyes as big as saucers.

Equinox Ego

My nightmare is like a message
from the eyes of dying horses.

Her body's foam splashed
from their overdriven flanks.

God's medium, she is larger
than the waking universe.

Her wisdom's all left-handed.
Her rider is Kafka.

Second sight, tarot pard –
her landscape is Escher,

and also roaring dust,
the fall of the House of Usher.

My nightmare's shoes were forged
from skeleton keys in the smithy.

Indeed, her trappings are spurs
still sparking as if on the anvil.

She gathers the homeless stars of grief
into the cottage of my ribcage

and her measures are the overreaching
darling hands of the dead.

VI

Antares

Song of the Émigré

We want to eat but there's blood in the bread.
The rioting crowd finds a fence to trample.
The phoenix is anaemic, the rivers are red.

Fashion dictates: dress yourself in lead.
Crows bestow unction in the pale temple.
We want to eat but there's blood in the bread.

Lights fail. Andromeda burns a hole in our bed.
A jazz song lacerates the night like a bramble.
The phoenix is anaemic, the rivers are red.

Sirens are the food with which terror is fed:
our thoughts in a knot that we can't untangle.
We want to eat but there's blood in the bread.

A man with a gun finds a woman to wed,
her *broderie* body a pattern of shrapnel.
The phoenix is anaemic, the rivers are red.

There's a curse on our country where every tread
takes you closer to death – that stale angel.
We want to eat but there's blood in the bread.
The phoenix is anaemic, the rivers are red.

Nemesis Depressed

All for edification,
there's one fury to unveil
the gore-flecked face,

and that obsidian egg yolk
the deep of the pupil,
fertilised ego.

Another to deliver
horror to the heart
of the suffering bystander:

sad-as-Psyche supplications,
while the victim kneels
before the holy knife.

The midnight comb falling
from my ash-blonde hair,
I love the victim –

and the villain too – their strife.
I press their hands together.
I'm their road to life,

their predetermined path,
their woad, their goad,
their *coup de grâce* – inked

with score and lore and sorrow.
I love every flagstone
where the furies dance,

dabbled with sacrifice,
the defile of soldiers,
the poison simple,

the blood-matted dewlap
dragged over the floor,
the gravedigger keeping

time in the groin –
my phial of nepenthe,
and my tongue on the coin.

The Angel Gabriel Advises the Rebel Leader

Capitán,

what your body needs, alas, is not you.
It's all infused with the incorrect person.

We see in your hand a tumbler of spirits,
tigerish sex down the alley (again),

your underwear sporting the last drying smear.
You will repair to the *Basílica,*
the *Sacerdote* who wears – mmm – *Dior Ambre
Nuit*. He will exorcise you, purple with incense.

Come back channelling medical doctors –
or even better a yoga instructor, tempered

with souls of terse dieticians. Only eat sushi.
Hold all that soy sauce and love avocadoes.

Organic. And blueberries, fresh from the season.
No more unreason and no more lewd dancing.

You will allow Mozart to block out your trauma,
flashbacks of being half beaten to death.

Enough of this Marxist and Leninist garbage;
Gandhi is nicer, the holy Lord saith.

Drop that Mars bar, and please quit the meth.

The Woman Ravaged Meditates on Hard

I live inside a broken piano.
Every dentist has the key to my molars.

My soul plays the mortgage on a smashed-up guitar.

The blunt rebels came with their axes and coshes
to beat the Beethoven out of my red socks,

to thrash through the wood of my Norwegian chords.
I'm nerve bear and greatcoat, dragging my blind skins

and bobbles through birthdays that burn to ground.

My e-strings, both snapped, have sensations of crocus.
Gibbering queenly, they are tendril and girl plait,

though, near the ice floes chinking at night,
tinkers with pokers might teach me to dance.

They cut off the hands of my dexterous player –
poetry's forged in sex, crows' teeth and pain.

My fingers, detached on a death row
of finches, nest on syringes, immortal wizards.

But who can say, with conviction, anything about birds:

they entertain harlots of henna and *chypre*,
have chrysoprase cities tattooed on their eyelids,

kumquats, a wire that runs to Spinoza.

So, spit out your pits, cherry snake of my song sheet –

Jesus, Eve genius, please say the word –
and run me home now on the through of your sword.

Three Spirits That Follow the Comet of Anguish

Spirit the First's mouth is a violet –
pentagram, petal and drawstring.

She kisses my head and sound caves in.
I'm deaf to everything but the banter

broken bone flowers lisp aloud in moonlife.
The goat ghost unravels her night kerchiefs

from tobacco pockets embroidered
with sinews, crocheted crow shade, her breath

an aftermath – of the rot, the dead bark –
horns and hornets in her bestial braids.

When she wipes my tears, my eyelids
dissolve and the sky comes through,

gros point of stars, moth on a cross,
chain gang Andromeda under my cough.

The final spook is one foot tall;
instead of heartbeats, bells in the chest.

She looks like a doll, preys in the breves
of demoted bay leaves, laurel amoral.

When the snow comes down
as broken glass,

in extremis jingles all the way –
the slain, the blood and the loss.

Philomela Unravels Nigeria

What hummingbird   has a machine gun
instead of a violin?

What flower desires   the bludgeon
as act of pollination?

Just so you know,   *I love you*
from now on will always   be vexed.

Never again   to be spoken
playful, exacting *yes*.

What has a machine gun,   hummingbird,
instead of a violin?

What bludgeon desires   the flower
as act of pollination?

Just so you from now on,   love,
know, I will always   be vexed.

Exacting to be spoken: never again,
playful *yes*.   Nightingale.

Butterfly Djinn

I am the blue clock's second hand yellow
butterfly – diurnal Balla blur of two antennae
effecting the Latin quarter of an hour while
I sip the nectar from *Made in China* typhoons
spiral out from the alarm bells and tickle
the Ali and Nino El Niño time flies in ambient amber

I remember visitors in the Eid of an evening
Eden the bluebell gazelles leapt up from the thickets
of a carpet to kiss our hands with noses
of crystallised rose petals and eat the proffered
sweetmeat of the prophet we played
Caliph and Heart's Desire going disguised
through the winding *suqs* finding djinn

and joy in the sherbet no sheiks
who didn't like Led Zeppelin and Deep Purple
Al Qaeda Darth Vader or Laura Croft Tomb
Raider smoke on the water we knelt on the flowers
that could never die or be deflowered casting
our thoughts like life ropes to Mecca
then we left Mom and Dad and Aladdin

we left Andrew Lang auld Peter Pan pixies Perrault
went out through the windows French into
an American bone garden
where there's Moon River riveted Damascus tense
wore on terror noon eyeless
no one's wireless in Gaza and no one laughs plays
nation shell shock's all nightmare and no punctuation

The Sky of Women: China

~ for Qiu Jin

The landmine was raked   by a husbanding housewife.
The red wine was spilt   onto her lap by a knife.

The house was husbanded   by a raking knife rape.
A wine wife was split   onto our laps by the landmine.

Can you marry a landmine?   Is your husband a knife?

The woman fort was worn   by a thorn called iron.

Qiu Jin, her comfort, keeps the pearl hues of poets in her spine.

Wear the comfort   being the thorn.
In my fort of pearl   I am the thought of iron.

Syrian Villanelle

~ *for Sea Watch and the Polish border refugees*

My wishbone breaks within my wounded breast.
In the foam of the sea, expectant women flail
for hope is a vacuum that nature detests.

Cold is the ocean blue infants ingest.
Tangled in seaweed is modesty's veil.
My wishbone breaks within my wounded breast.

Waves foam flippant with prayers on their crests;
a gale has mocked both the brave and the pale
for hope is a vacuum that nature detests.

There are things with scales in the optimists' nests.
Is hope a sparrow triumphant though frail?
My wishbone breaks within my wounded breast.

The border guards parade their bullet-proof vests.
The rescue-boat captain is crying in jail
for hope is a vacuum that nature detests.

They burn with cigarettes the souls that they arrest.
Blood and wet hair will dry out on the shale.
My wishbone breaks within my wounded breast
for hope is a vacuum that nature detests.

Nagasaki Deconstructed

~ after Yoko Danno

Mozart in a cherry
blossom, Sagami adorns
her hair with music.

Sei writes butterfly-
netting villanelles.
Flautist of the floating world,

Lady Ise kisses chiaroscuro,
long-necked lovers,
burnt sienna, water,

colour; then the bomb,
quaint as a catfish
hiccoughing an earthquake –

a cancer Chanel, a fell
message. This is how to fold
an envelope into everyone.

Acknowledgements

Thanks are due to the editors of the following journals in whose pages versions of some of these poems first appeared: *Adanna, Birmingham Arts Journal, Bull Spec, Coe Review, The Dawntreader, Errant Parent, Hollins Critic, Hunger Mountain, Jerseyworks, The Malahat Review, New Contrast, Off the Coast, Orbis, Other Poetry, PANK, Pennsylvania Literary Journal, Portland Review, Sein und Werden, Sharp, Signs: The University of Canberra Vice-Chancellor's International Poetry Prize 2018, Sounds of the Night, Third Wednesday, Yemassee Journal,* and *Zymbol.*

I would like to thank Warren Jeremy Rourke, Michèle Betty, Joan Hambidge and Helena Janisch for reading *Star Reverse* and giving valuable feedback.

I also wish to thank my friends Lestie Hughes, Leah Ndimurwimo and Barbara Kritzinger for being there for me through times good and bad. All my gratitude and love. May your stars move forever forward.

Linda Ann Strang

End Notes

Each part of this collection is named after a star, with the name being more-or-less relevant to the part's overarching theme: Zubenelhakrabi means 'in the claws of the scorpion'; Vega means 'falling'; Tislit is named after a lake in Morocco that is associated with two young people committing suicide because of the harsh decisions of their parents; Capella means 'goat'; Betelgeuse means 'the hand of Orion'; and Antares means 'opponent to Ares'.

Page 14

Aokigahara, also known as the Sea of Trees, is a forest situated beside Mt Fuji in Japan; many people go to commit suicide there.

Page 18

The title 'Enteric-Coated Nightmare 45' refers to the play speed of a vinyl single record, which is 45 revolutions per minute. Each section refers to a particular 45 record: Music Box Dancer, Both Sides Now (Clouds), and Mammy Blue.

Page 23

Ansel Adams was an American photographer, famous for his black and white landscapes. Pollux is a star in the Gemini constellation.

Page 27

The title 'Everything's Real Somewhere, They Say' refers to the popular interpretation of the Many Worlds Theory, itself an interpretation of quantum mechanics. The unitalicised lines in this contrapuntal poem, refer to the world known to us, while the italicised lines describe what is possibly happening in other versions of reality, in the multiverse.

Page 32

The poem 'Surreal Housekeeping, Good Advice' refers to the surrealist artists Leonora Carrington, Remedios Varo and Max Ernst. In World War II, Ernst was first detained as an undesirable alien by the French, and then later arrested by the Gestapo. Buddhist Pine, Wandering Jew and Zebrina are plants suitable for growing indoors.

Page 37

Héloïse d'Argenteuil was an abbess and woman of letters who lived in Europe in the 12th century. She is mostly remembered for her unhappy relationship with Peter Abelard, a philosopher, poet, and musician. Abelard, a proto-feminist, was castrated as punishment for his relationship with Héloïse. Abelard and Héloïse had a son, Astrolabe.

Page 80

'Philomela Unravels Nigeria' refers to the girls abducted by Boko Haram from Chiibok, Nigeria in 2014. Through the valiant efforts of many people, 164 girls were eventually released. But by 2021, 112 young women were still missing. According to Parkinson and Hinshaw in *Bring Back our Girls*, it is rumoured that some have died – in childbirth, from snakebite, and from undisclosed illnesses.

Page 82

Qiu Jin was a Chinese poet and revolutionary. An early feminist, she was beheaded in 1907 by the Chinese government. In one of her poems she wrote: 'My heart is far braver than that of a man.'

Page 84

Yoko Danno is a contemporary Japanese poet who writes in English. One of her poems, 'Catfish in the Woods', refers to the mythological Namazu, an underground catfish supposedly responsible for causing earthquakes.

OTHER WORKS IN THE DRYAD PRESS LIVING POETS SERIES

AVAILABLE NOW

Palimpsests, Chris Mann
Transcontinental Delay, Simon van Schalkwyk
The Mountain Behind the House, Kobus Moolman
In Praise of Hotel Rooms, Fiona Zerbst
catalien, Oliver Findlay Price
Allegories of the Everyday, Brian Walter
Otherwise Occupied, Sally Ann Murray
Landscapes of Light and Loss, Stephen Symons
An Unobtrusive Vice, Tony Ullyatt
A Private Audience, Beverly Rycroft
Metaphysical Balm, Michèle Betty

FORTHCOMING

Dark Horse, Michèle Betty
Night Transit, P. R. Anderson
earth circuit, Iyra Maharaj

OTHER WORKS BY DRYAD PRESS (PTY) LTD

River Willows: Senryū from Lockdown, Tony Ullyatt
missing, Beverly Rycroft
The Coroner's Wife: Poems in Translation, Joan Hambidge
Unearthed: A Selection of the Best Poems of 2016, edited by Joan Hambidge
and Michèle Betty

Available in South Africa from better bookstores nationwide
nd online at www.dryadpress.co.za, and internationally from African Books Collective
(www.africanbookscollective.com)

Printed in the United States
by Baker & Taylor Publisher Services